A native of Los Angeles California, Joyce Shintani pursued a career in conducting specializing in contemporary music until 1997, when she entered the music industry at Universal Edition Vienna and BMG Munich. When Napster brought the fusion and ultimate demise of BMG, she completed her dissertation on Gendertronics in Paris and taught 'music theory and aesthetics after 1945' at the University of Design Karlsruhe until her retirement in 2012. She remains active as author in Stuttgart.

Joyce Shintani

Hélène Cixous, *écriture féminine* and Musical Analysis

© Joyce Shintani 2016, joyce@joyceshintani.com

Publication by Lektorat-Bär, www.lektorat-baer.de, Stuttgart, Germany
ch@lektorat-baer.de
Corrections by Dorothée Leidig, www.textsieben.de

Herstellung und Verlag: BoD – Books on Demand, Norderstedt
ISBN 9783739247656

Cover design by Christian Bär using Photo © Olivier Roller and musical scores *Spices* (2001/2004) courtesy of Gerhard Stäbler and *AirBags* (2009) courtesy of Ricordi/Hal Leonard.

Unless otherwise noted translations, photos, and illustrations are by the author.
Cover quotation by Hélène Cixous refers to the complete dissertation.

Contents

Note to the Reader 7
Introduction 9
1. Exorbitant method: *Écriture féminine* 15
   1.1   History 18
   1.2   Topics 22
   1.3   Aspect: The 'Other' (*l'autre*) 23
   1.4   Aspect: What is 'feminine'? 24
   1.5   Aspect: Lacan 29
2. Reception in Musicology 39
3. *Lecture féminine?* 49
4. Bibliography 55

Illustrations

Figure 1 - Freud's Concept of Mind 32
Figure 2 - Constitution/Structure of the Subject (Ego, *moi*). 33
Figure 3 - Lacan's Borromean Knot 34
Figure 4 - Cixous' Seminar 53

Note to the Reader

This text, slightly revised and published here for the first time, was written as Chapter 2 of my dissertation, *Gendertronics. Toward A 'Lecture Féminine' of Emerging Musical Technologies and Their Aesthetics – Gerhard Stäbler, Terre Thaemlitz, Miss Kittin*, which was defended at the Université Paris-Est, France, in 2008.

To my satisfaction, extracts of the dissertation have already been published. Sections dealing with *métissage* of methods, the poststructuralist Subject, German notions of the Subject, and Gerhard Stäbler appeared in the *Revue Filigrane* (2010); and in the book *live · the opposite · daring* (2015) sections dealing with *métissage* of methods (again), with Stäbler's evolving musical Subject, and with an application of *lecture féminine* to his musical works were published.

Sadly, the thirty-odd pages I devoted to method based on the work of author and philosopher Hélène Cixous were left, so to speak, on the cutting room floor.

Inasmuch as Hélène Cixous' thought has not been widely applied to musical analysis, I have decided to publish these pages as a monograph that at once complements the already published material and also, with its bibliographical references, can serve as stand-alone introduction to Cixous and her work.

This makes parts of the dissertation available in three separate publications, small packets of digestible thought, but interrupts the original flow of ideas. Adventurous readers can find the first half of the dissertation in its entirety as pdf on my website www.joyceshintani.com.

Hélèn Cixous developed *lecture féminine* based on her theory of *écriture féminine* and used it to approach texts with students in her own seminars. It admits as equally valid the viewpoints of multiple readers and encourages the individual reader to arrive at conclusions from that multiplicity. Therefore, I have made wide use of quotations – different 'readings' – from which you, reader, may draw your inferences.

Each of the artists treated in the disseration has elements in his or her œuvre that make reference to elements of the theory of *écriture féminine,* thus making their work good examples for *lecture féminine.* These elements can be summarized as follows:

Changing concept of the Subject	Stäbler
Changing concept of musical material	Stäbler
Interstices of gender	Thaemlitz
Sex as weapon	Thaemlitz
Appropriation of means of production	Thaemlitz
(Bi-)sexuality	Thaemlitz
Rhizome subject	Thaemlitz
Corporeal electronics	Miss Kittin
Writing the body	Miss Kittin

After the methodological introduction published here, I intend to issue separately three remaining sections of *Gendertronics*: a history of electronica, a *lecture féminine* of work by composer Terre Thaemlitz, and one of DJ Miss Kitten.

My heartfelt thanks to Mme Hélène Cixous for her inspiration and for her kind permission to include previously unpublished notes here, as well as to Alan Hyde for his encouragement and challenging reading of my text.

Joyce Shintani
Stuttgart 2016

Introduction

> All biographies like all autobiographies like all narratives tell one story in place of another story (Cixous 1997e:178).

In previous writings, I have traced the paths within poststructuralism that led up to and point to Hélène Cixous' concept of *écriture féminine*. Here, it is neither my aim to furnish a comprehensive history of Cixous, her thought, or her works, nor to discuss their vast reception, as these areas have been more than amply covered by authors elsewhere.[1] An exception to this is the realm of musicology, which is treated in Section 2 below. My goal is to interpret Cixous' *écriture féminine* following the poststructuralist notion that there is no one, single Truth, only the interaction of different interpretations. The generous use of quotations here provides the reader with a spectrum of some interpretations.

Thus, I strive to communicate to you, my reader, my understanding of what *écriture féminine* can be: Looking at its historical influences, we will see what its themes are and how it can work. One of the characteristics of *écriture féminine* is its refusal to be defined. Hélène Cixous is clear from the very beginning:

---

[1] The reception of the French feminist theories in English began with articles that were almost contemporaneous with their appearance in the 1970s, and with books from the 80s onwards. The most prolific writer on Cixous is Susan Sellers (1988-2004); others include Conley (1984), Wilcox et al. (1990), Shiach (1991), Ives (1996), Cooper (2000), and Simon (2004). Among the most comprehensive early treatments of French feminism are Marks and Courtivron (1980) and Showalter (1985). The reception in Germany began later, drawing on the English texts to offer broad, systematized treatments, most often as part of feminist literary criticism or gender studies: Lindhoff, L. (1995), Osinski (1998). Cixous' original works were, of course, published in France, but it was only much later that they were received and appeared in anthologies there: Rossum-Guyon and Diaz-Diocaretz (1990), Negrón (1994), Calle-Gruber et al. (2000-2006). French systematic historic or critical treatments as of this writing [2008] have yet to appear. Countless dissertations have been written on Cixous and/or on *écriture féminine*. An excellent early literary treatment of Cixous' writing is Fisher (1988); the latest to my knowledge is Wardle (2007).

It is impossible at present to *define* a feminine practice of writing. And this impossibility will continue, for one can never *theorize* this practice, never enclose it, never codify it; which doesn't mean it doesn't exist. [...] This practice takes place and will take place in areas that are not subjected to theoretical-philosophical mastery (LM:883²).

Cixous found adequate places, *lieux,* to unfold her own *écriture feminine:* in literary works, often with unconventional forms, in the theater, and in her teaching activity. I offer here a historical orientation with a number of particular 'aspects', followed by a large number of 'topics' from *écriture féminine*. In my other publications on Gendertronics, many of the topics are thrashed out in discussions of musical works. But I begin with a few biographic elements, because for Hélène Cixous, what is recounted here

[...] (including what is forgotten and omitted) is for me inseparable from writing. There is continuity between my childhoods, my children, and the world of writing – or of the narrative (*Rootprints,* eng., pp. 203-204). Her speech, even when "theoretical" or political, is never simple or linear or "objectified", generalized: she draws her story into history (LM:881).

Hélène Cixous was born in 1937 in Oran in West Algeria, which at the time was still a French colony. The town of Oran had been founded in 903 by Moorish traders and was long under Spanish rule. Her father's family had "followed the classic trajectory of the Jews chased from Spain to Morocco".³ In 1831, Oran fell to the French. After the final bloody conquest of Algeria in the early 1900s, the French government confiscated communally held land, and European settlers moved in to farm it, a common practice of colonization. Prior to the Algeri-

---

² "Le Rire de la Méduse" in *L'Arc*, vol. 61, pp. 39-54; issue on "Simone de Beauvoir et la lutte des femmes" [Simone de Beauvoir and women's struggle]. English translation 1976 "The Laugh of the Medusa" [abbreviation LM in this text] by Cohen, K. and Cohen, P. in *Signs. Journal of Women in Culture and Society,* vol. 1, nr. 4, pp. 875-894, Chicago: University of Chicago Press.

³ The quotations concerning Cixous' background are from her book *Rootpoints*.

an War of Independence (1954-1962), Oran had one of the highest proportions of Europeans of any city in North Africa. Cixous' background, therefore, was a plurality of cultures. "When I was little I lived in a city full of neighborhoods, of peoples, of languages." But in addition, she says she had a "double childhood": Her father was a French citizen of Spanish descent; he was a businessman and played the violin. Her mother was of German and Slovak (Austro-Hungarian) descent. "Consequently, although I am profoundly Mediterranean of body, of appearance, of *jouissances,* all my imaginary affinities are Nordic." The German grandmother lived with the family, and Hélène grew up hearing French, Spanish, German, Arabic ... and her father forged "in a Joycian way" a play of signifiers and jokes on the German language "that became part of the family idiom.... Perhaps the verbal virtuosity or versatility that there is in my writing comes to me from my father." But her father is also a source of disturbance for her. A doctor, he contracts tuberculosis; and thereafter "there is a sort of veiled death in the house, the effects of which we receive only because my father reserves himself, physically, in his relations with us. He avoids holding us in his arms. This produces uninterpretable effects of distance for us."

When she was 18, she came to Paris to prepare for university studies; the Algerian War of Independence had just begun. In Algeria, Cixous had felt distant from her origins, "I was born so far from my beginnings". And as Jews under the French Vichy regime, even in Algeria, the Cixous family experienced anti-Semitism. But it was in Paris that Cixous experienced the new culture as an outsider, as a not-belonger, as an 'other'.

[In the Lycée Lakanal] I felt the true torments of exile. Not before. Neither with the Germanys, nor with the Englands, nor with the Africas, I did not have such an absolute feeling of exclusion, of interdiction, of deportation. I was deported right inside the class. In Algeria I never thought I was at home, or that Algeria was my country, or that I was French. This was part of the exercise of my life: I had to play with the question of French nationality which was aberrant, extravagant. I had French nationality when I was born. But no one ever took themselves for French in my family.

In the extract above, not only do we see Cixous' profound sense of exile, but also of her sense of urgency in dealing with her 'outsider-ness'. It became the exercise of her life, she *had* to engage with the question. The daily matter of feeling 'outside' necessitated her wrestling with the notions behind it. Inside, outside – it was her first large literary theme, one that later would be combined with sexual politics.

Soon after her arrival in Paris, Cixous met another Algerian émigré with whom she shared the feeling of being outside – socially and philosophically – until his death in 2006: Jacques Derrida. With geographical modification, Gustav Mahler's quote on exile could fit both of them: "Ich bin dreifach heimatlos: als Böhme in Österreich, als Österreicher unter Deutschen und als Jude überall"[4].

Cixous ended her study of literature in 1968 with a dissertation on the Irish author James Joyce, a figure for whom 'exile' was also a life topic[5]. In 1969 her first novel was published, *Dedans* [Inside]. In 1974, she founded the Center for Feminine Studies at the University of Vincennes (today Paris 8); it was the first institute of its kind in Europe. In the following year, she first formulated her literary theory of *écriture féminine*. In addition to her theoretical and instructional activities, Cixous has written numerous novels, poems and pieces for theater, the latter notably together with Ariane Mnouchkine at the Théâtre du Soleil in Paris. Today, following the practice in other countries, the institute has been renamed Center for Feminine and Gender Studies, and Professor Cixous continues her activities as writer and lecturer in retirement.

> The person we have been is now an 'I was', the character from our past. She follows us, but at a distance […] This is how I have behind me, one, two, three, four deceased women […] Left today is the one who will have followed us till here. And who passes with

---

[4] "I am thrice homeless: as a Bohemian in Austria, as an Austrian among Germans, and as a Jew everywhere."

[5] *L'Exile de James Joyce ou l'art du remplacement* [The Exile of James Joyce or the Art of Replacement]; Joyce's only play bore the title *Exiles* (1918).

me into the present. We cherish this one, the one who has traversed the decades where others fell: she cannot be, we believe, but the strongest and best of ourselves.[6]

---

[6] From *Jour de l'an*, (45-46), quoted in (Cixous 1997e: 138-139).

1. Exorbitant method: *Écriture féminine*

> Writing is precisely the very possibility of change, the space that can serve as a springboard for subversive thought, the precursory movement of a transformation of social and cultural structures. (LM:879)

We have cast a cursory glance at Hélène Cixous and how she became the person she is, and in a moment, we will turn to *écriture féminine* and the influences that shaped its contours. But before that, I resume the strand of another idea mentioned in the introduction: method.

A method, as we saw above, is part of a discipline aimed at discovering 'Truth'. A dissertation is an exercise that demonstrates the writer's learned ability to employ method to attain that Truth. If, however, I maintain that this Truth does not exist, for what do I need the method? And what, then, should the dissertation demonstrate, if not method? It is a fundamental conundrum for the deconstructive writer today. How can writing, a fundamentally logocentric activity, be conducted in an anti-logocentric – in an anti-phallogocentric – fashion? The answers to these questions may contribute to our understanding of *lecture féminine*, and Derrida gives us the first hint of an answer. In the preceding chapter, I explained deconstructive reading[7], but I did not yet mention that this kind of reading is an attempt to escape the ineluctability of logocentrism. Derrida refers to this attempt as "exorbitant":

> I wished to reach the point of a certain exteriority in relation to the totality of the age of logocentrism. Starting from this point of exteriority, a certain deconstruction of that totality which is also a traced path, of that orb (orbis) which is also orbitary (orbita), might be broached. [...] To exceed the meta-

---

[7] The historical treatment of deconstructive reading referred to is contained in the dissertation Chapter I Section 1.2 "Poststructuralism, Section 1.3 "Deconstruction and Phallogocentrism", and Section 1.4 "The Subject". The sections trace the development of the notion of Subject/author from its Cartesian roots through notions of Roland Barthes ("Death of the Author" 1967) and Michel Foucault ("What is an Author" 1969) to Derrida.

physical orb is an attempt to get out of the orbit (orbita), to think the entirety of the classical conceptual oppositions. (Derrida 1997e:161-162)
Disruptive questioning without hope of definitive answers as a way to escape the gravity of logocentrism. This is Cixous' point of departure. *Écriture féminine* is an ex-orbitary approach to writing; *lecture féminine* is an ex-orbitary approach to reading. Both are attempts to escape the orbit of fixed classical habits and oppositions. Thus, in calling *écriture* and *lecture féminines* 'exorbitant methods', I take up Derrida's oxymoron, recalling that their result is not the Truth. The reader who is accustomed to receiving morsels of Truth, packages of method and conclusion, etc., will be disappointed. As for my current endeavor, I wander on the crest between the academy and its deconstruction along with others of my generation. And we find *écriture féminine* on that path. It is exorbitant. And that, I find, is the reason Hélène Cixous is so adamant about the non-definability of *écriture féminine*, and one of the chief reasons it is so difficult to describe.

Hélène Cixous n'écrit pas sous la tutelle de la dichotomie chrétienne corps/âme, de la logique cartésienne et de la dyade aristotélicienne. Son écriture se meut dans les sentiers du non-connu, de l'errance et de l'imagination pure (Fisher 1988:5).[8]

A final remark on this *écriture féminine* as a 'method', drawing on the concept of 'nomadology' formulated by two other poststructuralists, Gilles Deleuze and Felix Guattari (1980n). Nomadology describes ways in which concepts – definable or not definable – fit into the accepted body of knowledge. The authors make a distinction between 'striated' and ‚smooth' space[9]. Something that is striated is characterized by striae, thin lines or bands, especially those that are parallel or close together; that is to say, structured. Striated space re-

---

[8] Hélène Cixous doesn't write under the tutelage of the Christian dichotomy body/soul, nor of Cartesian logic nor of the Aristotelian dyad. Her writing voyages on the paths of the 'not known', in meanders, and in pure imagination.

[9] Cf. Berman's description 2000:136-8. Abundant literature exists that discusses Pierre Boulez' concept of smooth and striated pitch-space and the Deleuze/Guattari concept.

quires endless vigilance and defense (gatekeepers and canons). Berman associates this with the *polis*.

Smooth space, on the other hand, is not structured; it follows the logic of the pasture (*nomos*). It is slippery. When threatened, an object in smooth space simply goes somewhere else. Since this space is about non-establishment, non-territory, there is nothing to defend.

The conflict between smooth and striated space can be seen in the history of science and art, as well as in politics. The smooth nomadic is not bound up into ruling hierarchy; the striated is. Calculus, for example, began as nomadic science with unruly notions of the limit and of the infinitesimal; the focus was almost completely on process, on becoming. State mathematicians sought to eliminate such nomadic notions and instead imposed static rules upon them; it became striated. The state always seeks to control the ambulatory and the heuristic, and this can be seen in everything from music to cathedral buildings. The model is that of a tribe in the desert, of relays and intermezzos, rather than that of a universal subject. This description of the slippery, smooth nomad – whether thought, writing, or art – reminds us of *écriture féminine*. It flies by, it is not susceptible to being theorized.

This brings us to the problem of institutionalizing or canonizing knowledge or, in our case, works of art. How to conserve, to sediment something whose nature is evanescent? Emergence. Perhaps this is what the composer often attempts. She cannot simply repeat the sedimented formula of the past, but seeks instead to give the listener an experience. The composer, almost like the alchemist, the proto-scientist, must create a re-creatable series of givens that, when reproduced, will produce a certain experience in the listener. At the moment the listener experiences the 'message', it 'emerges' in her brain. I believe this is what Barthes is referring to in the quotation from "Death of the Author" (1967:145): "There is no other time than that of the utterance, and every text is eternally written here and now".

Certain kinds of knowledge are not amenable to formulation. Rorty already noted this above by connecting Derrida to Ludwig Wittgenstein. And so, also, Berman's view: for Wittgenstein, "The true philosopher is not a member of any community of ideas" (138), he remains a nomad. Wittgenstein's admonition rings in our ears: "Wovon man nicht sprechen kann, darüber muss man schweigen"[10]; and "die Grenzen meiner Sprache bedeuten die Grenzen meiner Welt"[11]. And yet, as Cixous' quote heading this section counters, "Writing is precisely the very possibility of change, [... it is] the precursory movement of transformation". In writing, I expand my limits. I write, therefore, I am. No, I write, therefore I am becoming.

1.1 History

Écriture féminine, or feminine writing, has its roots in French post-structuralism and in feminist literary criticism, which developed as part of the international women's movement.[12] From the early 1960s onward, drawing upon their experiences in the nascent women's movement and in the sexual revolution, women proposed theories that would soon become compounded with ideas from poststructuralist thought. In the United States, feminists seeking equality through political and direct action developed theories of a pragmatic nature. New feminist journals, like *Signs, Feminist Studies,* and *Feminist Review,* provided ample place for formulating them.

Some years later in France, Luce Irigaray, Julia Kristeva, and Hélène Cixous began to formulate theories that directly engaged the thought of their poststructuralist milieu.[13] These literary or 'French feminist theorists', as they are referred to today, adapted post-structuralism to feminism. Linguistics, psychoanalysis, Marxism, and deconstruction all provided feminist critical theory with important analytic tools. However, due

---

[10] "What one cannot speak of, one must be silent about" (Wittgenstein, Preface, 1921: 9).

[11] "The limits of my language are the limits of my world" (Wittgenstein, §5.6, 1921: 67).

[12] The following remarks draw on accounts in Gamble (2001), Lindhoff (1995), Sellers (1991), and Showalter (1985), and the online lexicon *On Our Terms: A Feminist Lexicon. A Resource for Academics, Students, and More General Readers,* http://www.emsah.uq.edu.au/awsr/Publ_OOT/OOT.htm, as well as my own participation in the American women's movement from 1972 onward.

[13] Other theorists and writers who are counted to *écriture féminine* include Chantal Chawaf, Sarah Kofman, Annie Lèclerc, and Monique Wittig.

to the socially disrupting resurgence of the women's movement at this time, the form their work took was different from their poststructuralist colleagues and from their American counterparts. The French feminist theorists shared a common pool of thought and ways of thinking with the poststructuralists, but they treated areas not touched upon by their male colleagues, or treated them in different ways, often developing their own poetics. One of the most important themes they introduced into the poststructuralist discourse was the area of biology and body; for, structuralism silences the speaking body in favor of bloodless structures, and few poststructuralist theories suggest ways to articulate the body. There was, however, an animated exchange between the French feminists and the American authors and activists. American feminism was pragmatic – activist. On the other hand, the French were not so much concerned with what was said and done in their theory, but rather with the *process* by which meaning is achieved.

Showalter summarizes this development in three phases: first, becoming aware of sexual injustice in the women's liberation movement of the 60s and 70s; then, the discovery of the historical and thematic coherence of women writers and a rereading of literature; finally, feminist criticism that demanded a radical rethinking of the conceptual grounds of literary study and a revision of the accepted theoretical assumptions about reading and writing based entirely on male literary experience.

French feminist theory originated from one of the first and most influential of the groups founded by the feminist movement in France, *Psychanalyse et Politiques*, which established the influential publishing house *des femmes*. These feminists argued that differences between men and women are products of gender identities formulated through the operation of *discourse* rather than the consequence of biology; that binary oppositions are the dominant versions of sexual difference; and that theories such as Marxism, psychoanalysis, and poststructuralist thought could offer a way of deconstructing these oppositions: man/woman, rationality/hysteria, etc. Julia Kristeva, Luce Irigaray, and Hélène Cixous opened different perceptions and expectations to theory. Each one of these highly differentiated writers had her own particular view of language and her strategy for changing language and the meanings inscribed in it. Kristeva and Cixous consider that art and literature offer important evidence of the ways in which differences of thought are structured. Often allusive, poetic, and full of linguistic puns, French feminist thought is sometimes considered over-intellectual and 'difficult': however, the idiosyncrasy of their language is part of the poetics with which these writers seek a form of expression outside dominant structures of signification.

Écriture féminine is the result of this theoretical reflection, and it opened new creative possibilities. It is characterized by fluidity, fragmentation and *jouissance* (which means pleasure, including the sexual sense), and it is particularly associated with a *writing of the female body*. First described in Hélène Cixous' 1975 article, "*Le Rire de la Méduse* [Medusa's Laugh]", 'writing the female body' is one of its central concepts. But the essay is also a cry, a war cry in the name of *de-construction*, as is made clear in the third paragraph: "What I say has at least two sides and two aims: to break up, to destroy [**de**struction]; and to foresee the unforeseeable, to project [**con**struction]" (LM:875).

The seminal essay is, in the original, 17 pages long in seven parts, which correspond (but only very roughly) to the following topics: introduction; the suppressed feminine; breaking phallogocentrism by writing the body; woman's relationship to woman; bisexuality; grammar and what happens, when *she* writes; conclusion: love. The essay is truly seminal: the seeds of almost all the topics that Cixous would later develop in *La jeune née* (1975), *La venue à l'écriture* (1977), and other works are contained within it. She describes how women, through the means of writing, might break away from myths and rhetorical structures that have kept them from participating in society and in intellectual discourses. A form of feminist criticism, *écriture féminine* holds that there is an area of textual production that exists beneath the surface of masculine discourse and only occasionally comes to the fore in the form of disruptions of 'masculine' language. Particularly evident from the beginning was the desire to cultivate different points of view, rather than to develop one, specific method or theoretical system, a fact that makes grasping and reviewing feminist theory a slippery endeavor.[14]

---

[14] Tension is created in Cixous' superficially contradictory use of the terms

Julia Kristeva, drawing on Lacan, has summarized the latest phase of the feminist struggle (roughly since WWII, described above) in three steps. In the first, which she calls 'lib-'liberal feminism,' women demand equality of access to the Symbolic order (Lacan) – here we see the actions of the early American feminists. In the second step, 'radical feminism,' women subsequently reject the male Symbolic order, and femininity is extolled in the name of 'difference'; it is here that she locates the radical French feminists. In the third step, women recognize and reject the dichotomy between the masculine and the feminine metaphysical, a stance deeply nourished by deconstructive thought (Moi 1985:12). This is Kristeva's position, where Judith Butler might also be situated.

At the basis of the innovations made by the French feminist theorists was the notion of 'womanness' or *'féminité'*, the notion that only women possess certain characteristics. In this – at least superficially – essentialist notion of exclusivity, they unconsciously mirrored the behavior of 'clubby male exclusiveness' they had lived with for years. But in the evolution of their thought, these theorists developed their ideas, taking them beyond their initial stance. Their works, widely translated into English after 1985, experienced a landslide of positive reception in Anglo-American countries. It was not long before this point was recognized and commented on in yet another wave of theory, begun by Judith Butler's *Gender Trouble* (1990). In this reasoned critique of the preceding feminist thought, Butler also initiated a new appreciation of gender and performativity.

'writing the woman' and 'feminine'; reductionist thinking might see here biology vs. culture. While in "Medusa's Laugh" Cixous puts forth that "writing woman's body" is one of *écriture féminine's* central aspects (LM:880), she also cites men – Jean Genet and James Joyce (LM:878 and 884) – as examples of it. As Cixous points out below, these words are historical markers, not set terms. I find that the tension created by this seeming contradiction offers a bridge between the biological female (what came to be called essentialist) and the conceptual 'feminine', which would later prove fruitful for the development of gender concepts. This is also typical of how Cixous engages the reader to delve below the surface meanings of her words.

1.2 Topics

Cixous comes to writing via fiction. What relationship then does the 17-page long theoretical essay, "*Le rire de la Méduse*", have to the rest of Cixous' work?

> For me, theory does not come before, to inspire, it does not precede, does not dictate, but rather it is a consequence of my text, which is at its origin philosophic-poetical, and it is a consequence in the form of compromise or urgent necessity. Each time I have written or that I write a so-called 'theoretical' text – in quotations because in reality my theoretical texts are also carried by a poetic rhythm – it has been to respond to a moment of tension in cultural current events, where the ambient state of discourse – academic discourse, for example, or journalistic or political discourse – has pushed me to go back over things, to stop my journey and take the time to emphasize, to display in a didactic manner the thinking movement which for me was inseparable from my poetic movement, but which seemed to me to be entirely misunderstood, forgotten or repressed indeed by the topical scene. So all that is called 'theoretical' in my work is in reality simply a kind of halt in the movement that I execute in order to underline in a broad way what I have written or what has been possible to read for a long time in my fictional texts. (Cixous 1996)

This theoretical text, "carried by a poetic rhythm" and characterized by her typical word creations, sets out Cixous' program of *écriture féminine* and employs neologisms and concepts the reader may be unfamiliar with; it also redefines existing terms[15]. Most of these will be described and discussed individually in the context of the works to be considered in my other Gendertronics texts: bisexuality; difference/*différance*; feminine economy (including the 'gift' and the elimination of the 'masculine artifact'); *jouissance* (pleasure); perception; sex as

---

[15] "One has to take her texts as a mixture of theory and literature, for otherwise they are scarcely comprehensible" (Osinski 1998: 59).

weapon; subject (hierarchic binary opposition of subject/ object), and writing the body. But a few themes *underlie* the essay. To facilitate the procedure of preparing the reader for an individual *lecture féminine* of the works that follow, I will describe these underlying aspects that shaped *écriture féminine* and other texts of the time, as well: the notion of the 'other'; the notion of 'feminine'; and the psychoanalytic background touched on above.[16]

1.3 Aspect: The 'Other' (*l'autre*)

> The revelation which I [Cixous] believe to be the core of human experience: the nature of the relationship to the other (Cixous in Sellers 1988:143).

Next to philosophy, the notion of the 'other' has also been developed in the contexts of psychology (Freud, Lacan), feminism (Beauvoir), and social sciences (Said). It is generally understood as a contrast to or part of defining the self, a meaning it took on in Hegel's dialectics. I am my Self, s/he is the Other. In philosophy, Emmanuel Lévinas was instrumental in coining contemporary usage of 'the Other' as radically other (God). The term plays a role in the development of poststructuralism, as well as in French feminist theory. French theorists followed de Beauvoir's analysis of woman's construction as the 'Other' by seeking to explore the ways in which language and culture construct sexual difference, and to do this they drew on the work of the French psychoanalytic theorist Jacques Lacan. How does Cixous view the other?

> H.C. I could say that my first others are people of my family. Only if I move now into another, larger sphere, then I produce my other out of a sense of urgency. This other is imposed on me, is dictated in an absolute way to me, by history, by the state of history. Today it is necessarily women, the question of women, the woman. […] For me, the other is the other to love. Yet what I may have lived in my exist-

---

[16] Cf. Chapter I Section 1.3. "Deconstruction and Phallogocentrism", loc. cit.

ence was that the other had to be hated, feared, that he was the stranger, the foreigner, everything that is bad. I situate the other in what classically or biblically one could have called my neighbor. It is complicated to say this kind of thing. And then you have the whole range of others...
V.C. In that case, the other is not sexually determined. It could be any 'other'.
H.C. It is always anybody. (Conley 1984:144-45)

1.4 Aspect: What is 'feminine'?

On several occasions I have had the opportunity to speak of *écriture féminine,* and in 95% of the cases, the understanding of what Cixous means stops at the second word. People can't seem to get past the word 'feminine'. In her original manifesto, Cixous declared:

> Since these reflections are taking shape in an area just on the point of being discovered, they necessarily bear the mark of our time – a time during which the new breaks away from the old, and, more precisely, the (feminine) new from the old (la nouvelle de l'ancien). (LM:875)

We note here that the 'feminine' is *parenthetical*. Cixous goes on to declare,

> There have been poets who would go to any lengths to slip something by at odds with tradition...Thus did Kleist expend himself...

There are reasons to believe that where Cixous writes 'poet', we can also understand 'composer'.[17] Thus, obviously, we have every reason to look at the work of men with *écriture féminine* without 'feminizing' them (cf. Worth:438.) But this message has demonstrated itself to be extraordinarily difficult to get across! It is a fine line of demarcation that lodges the danger of misinterpretation for almost all. *Écriture féminine* **is not about writing by women!** "Attention ! Je n'essaie pas de créer une

---

[17] Cf. my discussion of the 'author' at joyceshintani.com.

écriture féminine, mais de faire passer dans l'écriture ce qui a toujours été interdit jusqu'ici, à savoir des effets de féminité. Je suis encore en état de recherche."[18] It is not even about femininity. It is about a type of writing with a gendered designation, gendered due to the historical context at the time of its description in 1975.

> For Cixous, the terms 'masculine' and 'feminine' do not refer to 'man' and 'woman' in an exclusive way. A clean opposition into man and woman would be nothing but a correct repression of the drives imposed by society (Conley:9).

Since this concept is apparently so difficult to convey, I will quote here lengthy extracts from "An exchange with Hélène Cixous" (Conley 1984:129-161), in which Cixous expatiates on what she meant and means with the terms 'feminine' and 'masculine'. It is the most succinct exposé by her on the subject I have found; moreover, it reveals many other nuances of her thought, such as philosophy, historical awareness, ethics, libidinal economy, her frame of literary reference, sociology, multi-level discourse, etc.[19] It is also an example for us to observe her style.

> H.C. The preliminary question is that of a 'feminine writing,' itself a dangerous and stylish expression full of traps, which leads to all kinds of confusions. True, it is simple to say 'feminine writing'. *The use of the word 'feminine' is one of the curses of our times* [my italics]. First of all, words like 'masculine' and 'feminine' that circulate everywhere and that are completely distorted by everyday usage, – words which refer, of course, to a classical vision of sexual opposition between men and women – are our burden, that is what burdens us. As I often said, my work in fact aims at getting rid of words like 'feminine' and 'masculine', 'femininity' and 'masculinity', even 'man'

---

[18] "Look here, I'm not trying to create writing that is feminine, I'm trying to get something into writing that has been forbidden up to now, namely the effects of femininity. I'm still researching" Cixous in Rambures (1978:58).

[19] Examples of exactly where and explanations of how Cixous uses these terms are given in Cixous 1997e: 157-160.

and 'woman', which designate that which cannot be classified inside of a signifier except by force and violence and which goes beyond it in any case. [...] Instead of saying feminine writing or masculine writing, I ended up by saying 'a writing said to be feminine or masculine', in order to mark the distance. True, it is a question here of our whole history, of our whole culture; true, it would be nice if one could use, instead of masculine and feminine, color adjectives, for example. Like blue and green and black [...] You see, these are linguistic instruments, words that do not take into account the reality of exchange...
When I read this text to you, I did not want to tell you at first who wrote it. Because if I do tell you, for example, that it is by Maurice Blanchot, I am saying that it is a text written by a man and you are sent back to the lure, to the screen. You are sent back to the fact that it is a man who wrote a masculine text. My own position is to insist always on the fact that libidinal femininity is not the *propre* of women and that libidinal masculinity is not the *propre* of men. What is most important for me, what allows me to continue to live and not to despair, is precisely the conviction that it does not depend on the anatomical sex, not on the role of man and of woman, but that it depends in fact on life's chance, which is everybody's responsibility. [...] Publicly, I must constantly have recourse to [strongly marked words], because we are in history, we live in history, we are in a historical, political situation which we must take into account [...] We must take into account the fact that we are caught in daily reality in the stories of men and women, in the stories of a role. That is why I come back to the question of the terms masculine and feminine. Why these words? Why do they stay with us? Why do we not reject them? Because in spite of everything and for historical reasons, the economy said to be feminine – which would be characterized by features, by traits, that are more adventurous, more on the side of spending, riskier, on the side of the body – is more livable in women than in

men. Why? Because it is an economy which is socially dangerous in our times. That is what we saw already with Kleist. You live, you believe, you give life to values that are apparently moral values, but in fact these moral values do not exist without precisely coming forth from a primary locus which is in any case *corporeal* [my italics]. If, for example, like Kleist, you believe in the possibility of a love, a real love, not one based on a power struggle, on a daily war, on the enslavement of one by the other, society is going to reject you. If you are a man, the rejection is almost immediate. Society does not give you any time [...] What you are doing is absolutely prohibited, and you are sent into madness and death. Women do have another chance. They can indulge in this type of life because by definition and for culturally negative reasons they are not called upon, they are not obligated, to participate in the big social fête – which is phallocentric – since they are often given places in the shadow, places of retreat, where they are in fact parked. It will be more easily accepted that a woman does not battle, does not want power. A man will not be forgiven.

V.C. Yes, but do women not want to get out of that negative historical position?

H.C. Something which is absolutely necessary. What I am saying is always on two levels. One level would be, if you like, that of libidinal truth. It is cut mercilessly by historical reality. I also say that for negative reasons, women have positive reasons to say something through generosity, which is mortal for men. Because man is projected on a scene where he has to be a warrior among warriors. He is assigned to the scene of castration. He must defend his phallus; if not, it is death. There you are. Women are not called upon the scene of castration, which in a way is not good for them, since they are repressed. Let us suppose that in our feminist period, women manage, for example to have equal chances; that is precisely where things start to become interesting and complicated. With equal chances, you are back in the old scenes. In the old scenes there were power struggles, and so what does one do? That is our problem. That is the problem of all women who, for example, cross the bar of absolute repression behind which women are parked and who are, in fact, on the side of men. What do they do? Either they are killed right away, or they effectively resist castration. They find themselves in the scenes where castration makes the law with the usual phallic stakes. But what about us? What we like, what we want, what men may also want but have been taught a long time ago to renounce – are we going to keep that? That is when one begins to live dramas. Are we going to be the equals of men, are we going to be as phallic as they are? Or do we want to save something else, something more positive, more archaic, much more on the side of *jouissance,* of pleasure, less socializable? If so, how and at what price? That is our daily question.

V.C. When you talk about 'women', even between quotation marks, you still refer to a very specific group with its demands and ideas of community. There are new exclusions, new masters.

H.C. The problem goes beyond that of women. It is the problem of any community, any society, because there have been many ideal societies. One collides right away with a contradiction that is *'not mastery'* [my emphasis]. I will take it at a banal level. When we founded Paris VIII, we founded it with the idea that there would be no more professors, no more masters – something that never did materialize, because if one is not the master, the other is, of course. We never did get out of the Hegelian system. What one can do is displace it as much as possible. One has to fight it; one can diminish the degree of mastery, yet without completely eliminating it. There always must be a tiny bit of phallus, so that things continue one way or the other. I believe that it is humanly impossible to have an absolute economy without a minimum of mastery [...] complete freedom, in my opinion, ends up by being too vague and is found only in spiritual evasion (extracts from 129-135).

1.5 Aspect: Lacan

In most mentions of *écriture féminine*, I have run across the importance of Lacan. Now, this may be true for Kristeva and/or Irigaray.[20] But, in my reading of Cixous I find very many – almost constant – references to Freud, not Lacan. L'enjeu en fait ne se situe pas exclusivement au niveau freudien. Au contraire, l'issue, la sortie, (les Sorties, pour plagier Cixous elle-même dans la Jeune Née) pour le sujet se trouve dans sa capacité de rejeter les théories freudiennes qui ne tendent qu'à déféminiser la femme, qu'á l'affaiblir ou la déposséder de sa puissance de corps (Fisher 1988:46).

Cixous worked with Lacan for two years[21], so we can assume she has some clear-cut views on him – the few remarks I found on him were very dismissive, for example on his (lack of) understanding of woman's *jouissance*[22]. Is it possible that many are interpreting Cixous superficially? Certainly, Cixous' very awareness of Freud and psychoanalysis might be traced to

---

[20] Let us not forget that both Kristeva and Irigaray *are* psychoanalysts (Irigaray was even expelled from Lacan's École Freudienne de Paris for her outspoken critiques of psychoanalysis), in contrast to Cixous. Kristeva's influential essay "Women's Time" (1981) deconstructs the binary opposition of masculine and feminine and opens up new notions of identity. For her, 'masculinity', and 'femininity' are particular socially constructed subject-positions and have little to do with biological difference. Irigaray found that psychoanalytic theory was not an analysis of patriarchy, but an example of it (Gamble 2001:176).

[21] "1963: For approximately two years she works regularly with Lacan" (Cixous 1997e: 210). In a letter to the present author dated "end May 2008", Mme Cixous wrote: "Je n'ai jamais été 'analysand' de Lacan, ni d'aucun analyste. (Mais lectrice de Freud, amie d'analystes – et attentive à tout instance aux effets de 'l'inconscient', et pour cause. Pas de littérature mais les souterrains). J'ai rencontré Lacan en 1963 parce qu'il cherchait quelqu'un pour l'initier à Joyce. Après quoi, nous sommes restés en amitié, chacun lisant l'autre. Il fut toujours convaincu que j'avais été analysée – preuve que - - - - à ma manière – Voilà 'moi – l'analyse' comme dit Derrida." [I was never the analysand of Lacan, nor of any analyst. (But a reader of Freud, friend of analysts – and always attentive to the effects of 'the unconscious', and with good reason. Not literature, but the underground.) I met Lacan in 1963 because he was looking for someone to acquaint him with Joyce. After that, we remained friends, each reading the other. He was always convinced that I was analyzed – proof that - - - - in my own fashion – voilà 'I – the analysis', as Derrida says."

[22] Cf. *jouissance* and Stäbler in Shintani (2015:123).

Lacan and the contemporary discourse, or to her actual discourse with him. True, her *écriture féminine* is 'based on pre-Symbolic Imagery' (Gamble 2001:177), and she emphasizes certain connections to the mother and to the origin and importance of language (Sellers 1991:44-64), but these notions may be attributable to both Lacan and Freud, to only one of them, or to a cocktail brewed of the two.

Cixous' post-Lacanian discourse, however, has also been indicted for supporting patriarchal and psychoanalytic norms. Ann Rosalind Jones and others have charged that underlying Cixous feminine economy, her sophistication in articulating it notwithstanding, is the assumption of an 'essential' femininity in texts, the identifiable quality that allows feminine discourse to be named as such in relation to Oedipus, the essential quality of openness that allows a text to resist external control and the superimposition of closed Oedipal patterns. More recently, however, other critics have come to her rescue [...] Anu Aneja has suggested that the case against *écriture féminine* results from a desire 'to locate *écriture féminine* within a definite category, a desire to co-opt into a literary theory that which always exceeds it' (1989:195). Aneja's observations place Cixous' discourse in relation to the Eastern doctrine of non-duality (Briganti and Davis 1994).

I have read of Cixous' 'neo-Lacanian', 'anti-Lacanian', and 'post-Lacanian' usages of certain notions. For my understanding, Lindhoff (2003) hits it correctly:

> The three most influential feminist theoreticians in France, Irigaray, Kristeva and Cixous, find very disparate consequences from Lacan's theory: While Kristeva follows the theory of Freud and Lacan in broad stretches, from which she develops a literature theory, Irigaray demands and practices psychoanalytic deconstruction of psychoanalysis itself. Cixous, on the other hand, who also employs Lacanian terminology, rejects intuitional psychoanalysis. (69)

A genealogy of those Lacanian thoughts that Cixous adopts but doesn't admit to, or that she deforms in using, exceeds the scope of this consideration. My reading suggests to me that Cixous may be performing her own interpretation of Freud, analog to Lacan's interpretation, as a *counterweight* to Lacan's; and that her standpoint does not depend so much on Lacan as on her own re-reading of Freud, giving her own emphases to themes like castration, libido and libidinal development, etc. After all, she did devote several works to Freud (on Dora) and to my knowledge, none to Lacan. Many authors do refer to this context, and manifestly, Lacan played an enormous and omnipresent role in preparing the way for poststructuralist thought. Nonetheless,

> The effect of Lacan in the women's movement is astonishing considering the fact that his theory restitutes a whole series of Freudian postulates. The central scandal of Freud's and Lacan's theories is the reduction of their theories to the male perspective; they are centered around the Oedipus complex, castration complex, and incest taboo, whose transfer to the female psychosexual development is problematic, to say the least. (Lindhoff 2003:70)

Since his notions on the development of the child – and particularly the feminist reaction to these – may not be familiar, I summarize for our discussion three topics from one area that are relevant: Lacan's notions of early childhood and personality development concerning a) the Subject, b) language, and c) the phallus. I follow here the description of Lena Lindhoff (2003:55-90), a description informed by feminist criticism, which was convincing in its detail and accuracy compared to other sources. Anglo-American authors no longer accord Freud and/or Lacan description in such detail[23]; but without such contextual detail, the aptness of the reaction of *écriture féminine* cannot be gauged.

Before we look at Lacan's revision of Freud, let us first recall Freud's theories concerning the formation of **subjectivity** and sexuality. Since I presume the reader is already familiar with these, I present them schematically with a few notes.

---

[23] I've even read on the American Musicological Society's forum that "Freud is dead".

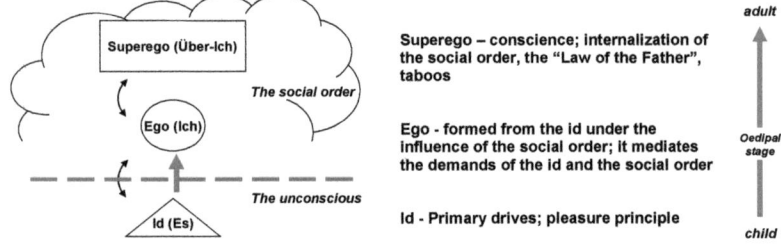

Figure 1 - Freud's Concept of Mind

Notes to Figure 1
- The formation of the superego takes place within the Oedipal stage – for Freud the crystallizing moment of early childhood development.
- The social order demands the repression of certain drives.
- The motivation for fulfillment of the ego is strengthened by the superego.
- The ego contains not just 'me and my desires', but also a critical parental eye.

Since Freud's theory is almost exclusively concentrated on the (male) oedipal complex and excludes the pre-oedipal phase, the male oedipal constellation (the incest desire toward the mother, the father-murder impulse, the father incest taboo, and the threat of castration) determines the content of the unconscious. Thus, Freud's theory of the psychosexual socialization is reduced to the male perspective. The patriarchal order of the family and society, within which the Subject is formed, is for him incontrovertible: a victory of the male spirit over the threatening, female connoted nature. Every deviation from this normal development is a mistake, and the woman has no own sexuality. As Irigaray puts it, "For Freud, there is no difference between the sexes: Humans are male; woman is a male without a penis."

Lacan turns around Freud's understanding of ego and unconscious: The true Subjectivity of the individual is to be found not in the conscious ego, rather in the unconscious. (Instead of *conscious* and *unconscious,* Lacan recognizes the imaginary ego (*moi*) and the true ego (*je*).)

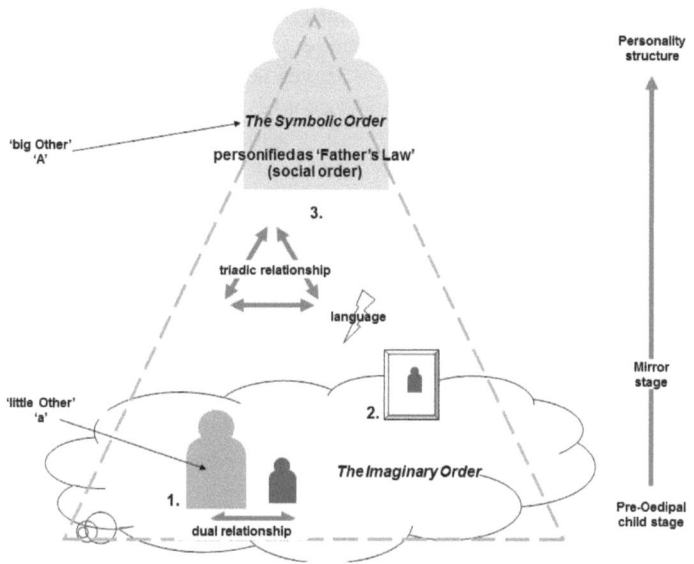

Figure 2 - Constitution/Structure of the Subject (Ego, *moi*)

Notes to Figure 2
1. We are in the realm of the Imaginary, the world of the first mother-child relationship. The mother and child have a dual relationship. As a child, the Subject's identity is not internal, it is external.
2. The mirror stage, the constitution of the Subject based on Hegel's master-slave dialectic, is accompanied by an ego-splitting, i.e., alienation. The child perceives its own specular image and acquires, through seeing its reflection, a sense of itself as separate being. It recognizes: "I am not the mother, I am me! But she is omnipotent!" In the mirror stage, the Subject tries to deny the split through an identity as autonomous ego within the mirror relationship. This denial, however, produces fear and aggression, since the Subject cannot be autonomous.
3. The recognition of being only mirrored, the realization of the alienation breaks through the structure of the Imaginary Order. Language enables separation from the mother. The child can

now enter the Symbolic Order, personified by the father. This recognition enables the Subject to replace the dual relationship with a triadic one, the third member being the social order. The Symbolic Order is inter-subjective; it is the origin of language and culture. The mother never leaves her position as projection of the male child; she never becomes a Subject; she cannot enter the Symbolic order. There is also a real world, which is represented in Lacan's Borromean knot:

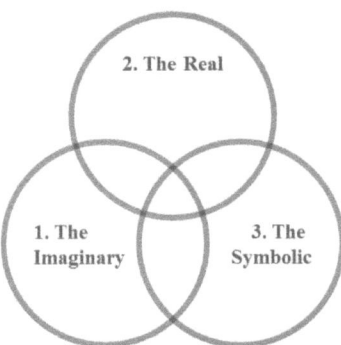

Figure 3 - Lacan's Borromean Knot

All later dual relationships of the Subject (man/woman, analyst/analysand) will be characterized by the original aggression of the mirror stage. The Imaginary, however, does not disappear after the mirror stage, it always remains as structure. The sexual roles are completely determined by the Imaginary. In love between man and woman, there is only one Subject: the male. The woman remains his selfless mirror.

So much for Lacan's theory of the constitution of the Subject. His notion of **language** is more complicated. Language is located in several areas: The origin of language is in the Symbolic order and language enables separation from the Imaginary order. The unconscious is structured like a language. The true nature of language can be seen and studied there. But language is a *dynamic* production of meaning, which is nourished by the inextinguishable desires of the (conscious) Subject. This desire is empty and seeks not objects, rather being and identity. The Subjects themselves are products of the linguistic production of meaning. But this social language is dead writing; it has lost its connection to desire. The social order is characterized by dead language. In contrast to this is the 'language of desire', a universal language. Simultaneously, this is the source of the Subject's individual specificity, which develops uniquely in every childhood: it is the *repressed* 'first language' of the Subject. This language is alive. Every person grows up within the Symbolic Order that determines everything. It is the patriarchal order, the 'Law of the Father'[24], that defines the structured patriarchal relationship of everything to everyone – the mother's body, the own body – the collective unconscious. The first language of the individual is thus the individual's own version of the incomprehensible patriarchal order. *Language in Lacan's scheme precedes all construction of reality.* Radicalizing Saussure's concept, Lacan speaks of a 'primacy of the signified'.

Signifieds (concepts of reality) are *'effects'* of signifiers (words). Language is not fixed (as by Saussure), it is rather a flowing, endless 'structuration' of signifiers (words). A word can have many other meanings, depending on its context among other signifiers. The concept 'glides' under a chain of words.

Lacan associates the endless movement of desire (which structures language and produces meaning) with 'metonymy'[25]. He associates the 'imaginary' fixation and hypostasis of mean-

---

[24] "In 1897 Freud remarked, on the basis of his analysis of his first patients and his self-analysis, that 'the father forbids the child from realizing its unconscious wish to sleep with his mother' (letter to Fliess, October 15, 1897). This first outline of the Oedipus complex, which now appears simplistic, grew increasingly complex throughout Freud's research. In time, the Law of the Father turned out to be directed both toward the mother ('You will not reintegrate your product') as well as her offspring swept up by desire. The law is also accompanied by an injunction against cannibalism and murder, and holds up ideals, primarily sexual ones ('Later you will enjoy, like me, a woman from another family'). Once introjected, this becomes the origin of the superego and ego ideal. The repression of drives, their suppression and sublimation, are the principal outcomes of the conflict that connects them structurally to this law." Article "Law of the Father" in Locklear, S. (2005) in Mijolla, A. (ed) *International Dictionary of Psychoanalysis,* English version, Farmington Hills MI: Gale Group and eNotes.com (2006), retrieved: 14 Sep 2007.
http://www.enotes.com/psychoanalysis-encyclopedia/law-father.

[25] A figure of speech in which one word or phrase is substituted for another with which it is closely associated, as in the use of 'Washington' for the United States government or of 'sword' for military power.

ing with 'metaphor'[26]. But, in the last analysis, metaphors are based on metonymies. These two basic principles of language function are different, but inseparable. Accordingly, the notion of the 'imaginary' is ambivalent. On the one hand, the imaginary is a basic function. The structuring identification of the developing Subject in childhood is a necessary pre-condition for grasping reality. On the other hand, the 'imaginary' constitution of ego and the world is a process of the acquisition of reality – with a negative result: the ego and its objects become *fixed* in a narcissistic (phallic) construction.

We have reached the third apsect to be considered here. In the formation of Subjectivity and language, the **phallus** plays a central role. According to Lacan, in the mirror stage, the child believes the mother is 'phallic'. The child then recognizes, however, that the mother is 'castrated'. The child doesn't assume that the mother is simply different, she is castrated. Previously in identity-union with the mother, the child now makes its first discovery of non-identity – and denies it. The missing phallus becomes the child's fetish, he must have it. It is the first imaginary object of the child (*objet a*) that serves to hide the experience of difference behind an assumed identity.

Precisely this is the function of language. The phallus stands [!] thus at the beginning of language, it is the 'first signifier', and language is nothing but an endless process of the constitution of imaginary objects destined to fill the fundamental lack of identity, which characterizes all human existence. All terms of language are only new substitutes for the phallus. It is the connection to the unattainable 'real'. The order of language creates autonomous identities, where in reality there is only interaction and difference. Finally, there is the father. The 'Symbolic father' is language itself, which precedes all individuation as an impersonal authority. It is the 'Law' or the 'big Other'. Language delivers salvation to the Subject. It enables self-identification and corrects narcissism.

We are nowhere near the end of Lacan's theories, and I have not yet expounded those that derogate women, but we

---

[26] A figure of speech in which a word or phrase that ordinarily designates one thing is used to designate another, thus making an implicit comparison, as in 'a sea of troubles' or 'All the world's a stage'.

have enough to get a good impression of them, to help us identify them in Cixous' writing, and to help us imagine the reactions they provoked. In reading them, we notice first how distasteful they are to women, as well as to men today. The violent responses of Cixous and others become understandable and justified – they are the existential struggle for woman's own identity and sense of self. At the same time, just as the French feminist theorists in the 1970s, we today stand in awe of a fine network of theories that covers so many areas of intellectual history, human existence, and cultural creation. How could one not be seduced by some of Lacan's ideas on the origin of language?

Through Kojève, Lacan had assimilated Hegel's thought, and we see it here, illuminating his reading of Freud. In Freud's image, the poor Ego, like a meatball in a sandwich, was caught between one slice, pressing down on him from above – his internalized societal superego – and his slice of primary drives pressuring him from below. The poor meatball is deemed healthy if he manages to keep control. Lacan also sees the ego caught between forces, but views personality formation and structure as a dialectic process. By introducing the element of language as the dynamic motor in the process, language becomes the royal jelly that enables the ego, relaying between the pressures, to construct itself and even reality, not merely still its drives. It is the creation of the imaginary sublime – for pleasure's sake. Here, the notion of *Aufhebung* is reflected in this true dialectic that always reaches a new plane. Indeed, Lacan's image reflects more accurately what we know today about the way the neurons of the brain work together in processes of perception and ratiocination. Cixous' *lecture féminine* will take this image yet another step closer to the empirical models of the brain's functioning we know today, so many years later.

The pure beauty of Lacan's notion must have delighted the aesthetic perception of his readers, captivated them. The gigantic structure of his thought galvanized the brilliant postwar generation of young scholars and intellectuals who were forging a new identity for Europe out of the ashes of the Second World War. Lacan's thought served either as a reference point to be accepted, rejected, or continued; or as a lever to stem the weight of new, emerging theories, critiques, and refutations, as in the case of Cixous and the French feminists theorists.

It is this view of sexual difference as constructed in and by language that influenced the development of French feminist theory. In their different ways, Irigaray, Cixous, and Kristeva sought to establish a female identity, language, and writing which would subvert and/or deconstruct the phallocentricity of the Symbolic Order. In so doing, they opened up for feminist investigation questions about the relationship between desire and language and about the constructed nature of identity (Gamble 2001:40-41). "Lacan is an antifeminist thinker who gave feminism a new foundation" (Lindhoff:78).

With this contextualization, I close the résumé of poststructuralist topics of particular relevance to our discussion of *écriture féminine*. I now turn back to Cixous and to the reception her works have received in the realm of musicology.

2. Reception in Musicology

Although Hélène Cixous has enjoyed abundant reception in disciplines such as literature, feminist theory, gender studies, and psychology, her theories have seldom been approached by musicology and media theory and, with one exception to my knowledge, not at all with regard to multimedia. In reference to opera and/or the voice, some authors have mentioned *écriture féminine en passant*, but without in-depth treatment.[27] Three musicologists who have taken on large presentations are Joke Dame (1994), Hanna Bosma (1997), and Sanna Iitti (2006), who have all argued for a kind of musical *écriture féminine*.

To my knowledge, the first person to apply Cixous' *écriture féminine* to music in an extended work was Dutch musicologist Joke Dame in her dissertation, later published (1994) as *Het zingend lichaam. Betekenissen van de stem in westerse vocale muziek [The Singing Body. Significance of the Voice in Western Vocal Music]*. Since I cannot read Dutch, I must rely on statements made about this book by the next person to treat the topic, her compatriot, composer Hannah Bosma. In 1997 the latter wrote:

> In her book *Het zingend lichaam,* Joke Dame suggests a similarity between the literary work of French women writers (such as Hélène Cixous) under the name of *écriture féminine* and music by composers like Luciano Berio and John Cage. Even more so, Dame proposes to consider as *'écriture féminine musicale'* the vocal music of Cathy Berberian, Joan La Barbara, Meredith Monk, Diamanda Galas, Laurie Anderson, Moniek Toebosch, Greetje Bijma and

---

[27] An early, short presentation is Lorraine (2001), a 15-page article that represents the first section, "Feminine Aesthetics", in Pendle's *Women and Music*. (The first edition appeared in 1991, so presumably her article dates from then.) The article attempts to localize possible 'feminine aesthetics' and is a remarkable *tour d'horizon* of theories at the time. Lorraine devotes only two pages to Cixous, Kristeva, and Irigaray and doesn't quite succeed at separating entirely the treads of their different thoughts; thus, the use Kristeva and Irigaray make of Lacanian precepts are mixed with Cixous' stance.

Jannie Pranger. However, Dame does not further work out this interesting suggestion [...]
In her suggestion of an *'écriture féminine musicale'* Dame stresses the vocal, non-verbal, non-linguistic aspects of *écriture féminine:* close to the voice, the voice of early childhood and the voice of the mother, the body, the flesh and rhythm of language, play, disruption, excess, gaps, grammatical and syntactic subversion, laughing. The idea that feminine vocal music is characterized by the use of nonverbal, prelinguistic voice sounds is also offered by Renee Cox [Lorraine; cf. note above] in her article "Recovering Jouissance".

Both Dame and Cox relate these aspects of *écriture féminine* to Kristeva's notion of the semiotic, that consists of the materiality of language, sound, the sound of the body, the movements of the voice, intonation, timbre, [and] rhythm that accompany and disturb language. Kristeva's 'semiotic' is linked to the pre-linguistic, pre-symbolic, pre-oedipal primary processes.

According to Bosma's description, Dame takes a first step in joining approximately contemporaneous music with *écriture féminine*. I note three aspects in her description. First, Dame senses the proximity between *écriture féminine* and composers who found completely novel areas of music like Cage. Second, Dame brings *écriture féminine* into proximity with vocalists who have utilized a great deal of bodily engagement and/or who use a great deal of improvisation. She is certainly 'on the right track': It is a proximity that all following interpreters will take up – the logical, sensitive first step, in my opinion. Finally, Dame takes up the notion of pre-linguistic sounds. As we saw above, this notion of Lacan localized the 'feminine' in the premature, 'pre-symbolic' phase of development. "However, Dame does not further work out this interesting suggestion." It is now up to Bosma, for she is the next to take up the topic.

Dame's notion of *écriture féminine musicale* evokes questions about the relation between this 'feminine' music and the, predominantly male, musical avant-garde. Also, questions arise concerning the role of language, voice, body, and electronic sound technology.

All vocalists and composers mentioned by Dame not only used the voice, but also electronics.

In her research for her own doctoral dissertation, Bosma poses more specific questions than Dame did, probing deeply into the matter of the voice.[28]

I want to focus in this paper only on the idea of the pre-linguistic voice as feminine. So I will not discuss other possible aspects of *écriture féminine musicale*, for example related to musical structure [...] The idea that women have a privileged relation to the pre-cultural, pre-linguistic of pre-symbolic realm is a common stereotypical idea in our culture. *Écriture féminine* reinforces, elaborates, and extends this idea. Instead, I do not relate femininity to the general notion of a presumed uncultural body. I consider feminine practices such as mothering and singing as cultural practices of women. In the work of female vocalist-composers and of women composers, I perceive a mixture of masculine and feminine cultural practices, such as singing, composing and electronic sound technology; and often I find in electrovocal work of women composers references to cultural feminine issues like mothering and singing.

Thus, we see that Bosma restricts her prime concern to pre-linguistic voice (representing the feminine) and particularly investigates the area of electrovocal music and composing, her main areas of personal occupation. Here, Bosma becomes quite concerned with ticklish questions on the nature of what is feminine and what is masculine. Bosma also takes up Dame's treatment of Berio with regard to *écriture féminine* and after an analysis of *Thema - omaggio a Joyce* for tape (1958) formulates the question, "Is Berio a feminine subject?" and comes to the resounding negation, "I would say no: Berberian's work was appropriated by him. There is no place for two different authors of *Thema* in its surrounding dominant discourse."

---

[28] Dame treated this topic in her article "Unveiled Voices. Sexual Difference and the Castrato" (1994) in relation to Barthes, but not in relation to *écriture féminine*.

The third person to do extended work on *écriture féminine* with regard to music is the Finnish musicologist Sanna Iitti. In her 2006 book, *The Feminine in German Song,* she develops her own theory of musical gestures based on Cixous' *écriture féminine*. Her work has two foci: a) determining the gender of works, which entails defining and discussing historical notions of feminine and masculine; she recognizes feminine qualities in both male and female individuals and undertakes the fine distinction between men's and women's femininities; and through this, she seeks b) to enable a new, non-hierarchical view of music and its forms, particularly in the 19th century. Iitti offers extended, multi-facetted philosophical discussion of Cixous' concepts. She accepts the viewpoints of Lydia Goehr (1998) and Nelson Goodman, but refutes Lorraine's interpretation (1991), claiming that Lorraine failed to recognize the proper epistemological context of Cixous thought, Derridean deconstruction, and asserts her own interpretation:

> Feminine writing should neither be treated as a prescription for a particular style, nor equated with "women's music" in an essentialist manner. Ignoring the fact that Cixous identified *écriture féminine* in multiple historical contexts led Cox Lorraine astray. French post-structuralist theory nevertheless allows us to explain musical constructions of gender, regardless of the composer's period or sex. A Cixousian approach to music and gender must posit *desire*[29] as the generative principle of musical production. *Écriture féminine* is motivated by the feminine libido, denied by Freud. It suggests spontaneous musical creation and refers to improvisation and tone color. Historically, as composers, men transgressed their customary gender roles in society, thereby acquiring freedom. Women's feminine expressions nevertheless perpetuated devalued genres. Feminist musicology should therefore uncover the emancipating potential of gender studies in music. Analytically,

---

[29] My emphasis. I recall the discussion above of how, in the emerging post-structuralist conception, desire helps constitute the Subject. I will continue this discussion in the chapter on Stäbler, published elsewhere (cf. Introduction).

this suggests going beyond the score and engaging factors that emerge in performance but cannot be notated [...] actual gestures in performance. (Iitti 2003 and cf. 2006:19)

We sense here how Iitti is building her argument for a reevaluation of 'women's' small musical genres in the book and for a beginning valuation of performance gestures. To accomplish this, Iitti goes on to unfold a minute investigation of feminine constructs in the 19th century, their history, and their manifestation in music. In effect, she deconstructs them, always referring to Cixous.

In contemplating *écriture féminine,* both Bosma and Iitti dwell on definitions of feminine and masculine in order to try to find evidence of the one *écriture* or the other. While in no way do I put their academic methods into question, I personally find this approach a dead-end street. No sooner have I found some 'feminine' writing than I discover possible 'masculine' attributes. And when I start examining 'men's femininity', at some point all defining characteristics seem to become arbitrary. Like Saussure's signifiers. In the last analysis, the pair of binary opposites 'masculine/feminine' bears within it the very hierarchy that *écriture féminine* avows wanting to go beyond.[30]

Although my focus lies outside of areas these three authors deal with, nonetheless I can only heartily welcome the growing attention and depth of investigation into this broad theme. In my reading of them, the steps they take are pioneering and timely. They have an inner consistence and reflect music history and theory as well as the broader philosophical context. Each of the authors presented in this section, including the following, took the integral 'next-step' in the musical reception of Cixous' *écriture féminine.* My work is another step, and I hope that all these steps will continue. It is a project, like deconstruction, that will go on and on. I thank these authors for the intellectual simulation they have given me.

To conclude this section, I come to a fourth writer, whose short article takes the direction of my own thought, quite possibly because it is the most recent and because it deals with the

---

[30] Cf. Cixous' concept of bisexuality in the dissertation section on Terre Thaemlitz, to be published separately.

same musical matter I do: multimedia art. In 2005, curators Lina Dzuverovic and Anne Hilde Neset organized the huge exhibition *Her Noise* at the South London Gallery with satellite events at the Tate Modern and the Goethe Institute London.[31] The catalog contains an excellent overview article by Christoph Cox, *"A la recherché d'une musique féminine"*, concerning women's often ambivalent feelings toward having their art be treated as 'women's art'. He names the often drawn distinction between 'egalitarian feminists' (or essentialists) and 'difference feminists'.

> Among difference feminist, theorists such as Hélène Cixous, Julia Kristeva, and Luce Irigaray searched for an *écriture féminine,* a uniquely female mode of writing[32] characterized by a joy in the materiality of language, multiplicity of voice and linguistic register, and a fluidity and duration that resists closure and remains in media res […]
> Is there a *musique féminine,* a noise that can rightly be claimed as hers? Artist and theorist Dan Graham grapples with this question in an important essay from 1981. Titled "New Wave Rock and the Feminine", the essay examines a range of positions that have been available to, and strategies that have been taken up by, women in pop and rock since the 1960s. […] the heart of his essay: an analysis of sexual difference and female specificity.

Cox, too, dwells on defining 'feminine' elements, quoting artist Dan Graham (1993) extensively in his quest to locate these.

> Drawing on the heterodox psychoanalytic framework that informs the writing of Cixous and Kristeva, Graham locates the feminine in a kind of return of the repressed: in a resurgence of the primary drives that have been foreclosed by entrance into symbolic language, the establishment of a stable ego and the regu-

---

[31] http://www.ubu.com/film/her_noise.html.

[32] As we saw above, for Cixous, *écriture féminine* is not uniquely female; Cox notes this himself below.

lation of sexual desire. Never integrated fully into the symbolic order, argue Cixous and Kristeva, women have privileged access to these primary drives. For Graham, this resurgence finds its musical manifestation in extreme expressions of the female voice.

Once again, the tropes of repressed desire, the Symbolic order, and the importance of the voice are labored. But, Cox and Graham find some other interesting characteristics, which recall aesthetic elements Eva Rieger (1992)[33] once listed as typical of classical music composed by women.

> More generally, Graham discerns this female specificity in music that is 'plurivocal, heterogeneous and polymorphous' [...] Exchanging instruments and roles after every song [creates a] 'non-hierarchical structure' that undermined stable group identity and identification with the singer/hero. Likewise [... the] 'deliberate use of mistakes, silences, and personally motivated or arbitrary shifts of pattern/feeling' that produced a musical texture characterized by a 'continually shifting, polyvalent, hierarchical pattern'.

Cox continues, "Graham's argument is powerful and intriguing. Yet surely such characteristics are not unique to all-women or women-led groups". Certainly not, Cox affirms, going on to list male artists who share these characteristics.

> Yet, just as Cixous and Kristeva champion James Joyce, Jean Genet, Antonin Artaud and other male writers as exemplars of *écriture féminine,* so we might see these male musical precursors as fellow travelers in the project of resisting or undermining the structures of sexual-social power that pervade music and musical organization.

And now Cox hints at the new direction his thought takes him, along with Reynolds and Press (1995):

> 'Having exhausted the psychosexual dynamic of male rebellion', writes Reynolds with Joy Press,

---

[33] Quoted in MacArthur (2002) *Feminist Aesthetics in Music.* MacArthur's view: "The central argument of this book is that women's music operates according to aesthetic criteria that suggest differences from men's music" (173).

'rock culture is confronting the possibility that the only new frontier is the specifically female experience that has hitherto been left out of the script.'

Suddenly, we are not talking about aesthetics. We have shifted to 'the experience'. What is this specifically female experience? Where are the great female sonic wizards?

The answer lies outside the rock fortress in the domains of experimental and electronic music, where women have played a prominent role for nearly a half-century. Although entirely ignored by [standard texts] on the subject, pioneers such as Pauline Oliveros, Maryanne Amacher, Alison Knowles, Maggi Payne, Laurie Spiegel, Annea Lockwood, Eliane Radigue, Christina Kubisch, Meredith Monk, and Ellen Fullman have produced work as significant as their male counterparts […]

For Oliveros[34] and her generation, electronics opened up a new and uncharted world. Beyond the ordered, stratified[35] domain of music, it gave access to what John Cage called 'the entire field of sound' and what media theorist Friedrich Kittler has called 'acoustic events as such': no longer merely pitches, scales and meters embroiled in formal systems of meaning and communication, but all the noises of the world in all their messy heterogeneity laid out on a single plane. Kristeva calls this plane 'the semiotic'; and philosophers Gilles Deleuze and Félix Guattari call it the 'body without organs'[36]. All three maintain that it has a unique resonance with the feminine. For Deleuze and Guattari, the liberating transformation of the human subject and of music into a body without or-

---

[34] Pamela Madsen (1994) explores the notion of 'feminine form' in Oliveros' deep listening (my footnote).

[35] Cf. nomadology above.

[36] Stevie Meriel Schmiedel offers comprehensive and easily understandable genealogies and explanations in his *Contesting the Oedipal Legacy. Deleuzean vs. Psychoanalytic Feminist Critical Theory* (2004), to which I will refer below. Concerning rock music and gender see also Riley (2004) *Fever: How Rock 'n' Roll Transformed Gender in America*.

gans first requires a 'becoming woman', a dismantling of the libidinal investments that characterize Man and Music as norms, and the cultivation of a broader range of affective relationships. From this perspective, experimental electronic music signals the becoming-woman of music; and women have a privileged relationship to musical experimentation. Here, women do not follow but lead. And this *musique feminine* offers a glorious world of noise that is hers and, via his becoming-woman, man's as well.

Who would ever have thought that woman's oft cited multi-tasking capacity to create order out of a chaotic babble of children at the family hearth – "all the noises of the world in all their messy heterogeneity laid out on a single plane" – would one day be perceived as having a particular "resonance with the feminine"? I understand Olkowski's critique of Deleuze's standpoint (cf. Chapter on Thaemlitz), and following her, I doubted the necessity of Deleuze's new concept 'becoming-woman' to express this philosophically – until a respected feminist male colleague countered my skepticism with, "Why not? That's what I needed in order to get in touch with my feminine side." Thank you, Christoph, for pointing your finger in the direction I see *écriture féminine* indicating today. It is a standpoint that opens up a path of 'together'. It is the path that both Deleuze and Cixous point to. It is neither **a** woman's direction, nor **a** man's direction; it is our direction, of us all, as we walk experimentally and experientially together into a very uncertain future. Cixous wrote of woman's place in the shadows, where experimentation is easily accepted. If this is what it takes to arrive at the insight that "women have a privileged relationship to musical experimentation", then I can only say, *"Allez-y!"* – or better still, *"Allons-nous!"*

3. Lecture féminine?

> The non-master must be imagined. (Cixous and Clément 1986:144)

Till now, I have described feminine *writing,* and now we turn to **lecture** *féminine,* or feminine *reading.* If "Rousseau inscribes textuality in the text" (Derrida), the artists I treat attempt to inscribe their meaning everywhere but in text, and it is with the 'exorbitant method' of *lecture féminine* that we hope to decipher these attempts – bearing in mind Barthes' caveat above: "Once the Author is gone, the claim to 'decipher' a text becomes quite useless". How did we get from one to the other?

Since founding her Center for Feminine Research in 1974, Cixous has sought with her students to arrive at a new kind of textual explication: feminine reading. She criticized the then current fashion of reading texts "on a purely formal level"; in contrast, she proposed a new kind of reading:

> "The texts we work on are strange either because of their language or because of what they say. What binds us together is our belief in the need to ensure that the essence of each strangeness is preserved [...] There are thirty ways into a text. Reading together in this way we bring the text into play. Though work on the form is necessary, it doesn't uncover the heart of a text. We take a page and everyone comes individually towards it. The text begins to radiate from these approaches. Slowly, we penetrate together to its heart."[37]

Even male literary critics were apprehending the necessity for a new kind of reading. Stephen-Paul Martin wrote about feminine reading in 1988:

---

[37] Sellers 1991: 143-148. Further references on this topic are Part 4, "Teaching after Cixous" in Wilcox, H. et al. (1990) *The Body and the Text. Hélène Cixous, Reading and Teaching,* and the chapter "Coming to Reading Hélène Cixous" by Deborah Jenson in Hélène Cixous (1991) *"Coming to Writing" and Other Essays.*

> Up until very recently, men in Western cultures were encouraged to be arrogant in their pursuit of power and pleasure, to assume that they had the right to penetrate and subjugate whatever they wanted to enjoy or possess. But when we "penetrate" an experimental text, such phallocentric arrogance is inappropriate. Because the work will not be immediately accessible, it will ask us to approach it with much more respect than men are expected to display in most business or professional situations. [...] Once the desire to inseminate the text is activated and we have shared our masculine potency, feminine energies assume primary importance. Although an initial investment of masculine attention is necessary, the processes of gestation, pregnancy, birth, and nurturance are more significant in dealing with open literary structures. Instances of how this works might be found in the tendency of contemporary writers like Derrida, John Cage and Jackson Mac Low [...] Students have always been taught to read like men and *penetrate* the work. What they have not been taught is how to create and nurture it (10-11).[38]

It is important to remark, however, that indications can't be taken too literally. For on the one hand, the interpreter is tempted to apply Cixous' formulations superficially; on the other hand, Cixous doesn't want her descriptions to be taken as rules.

> I choose to work on the texts that 'touch' me. I use the word deliberately because I believe there is a *bodily* relationship between reader and text [...]. We listen to a text with numerous ears [...] Every text has its foreign accents, its strangenesses, and these act like signals, attracting our attention [...] We aren't looking for the author as much as what made the author take the particular path they took, write what they wrote. We're looking for the secret of creation, the same process of creation each one of us is

---

[38] In the section "A Polemic for New Reading"; my emphasis. Compare his remark on penetration with Barthes' above in the section 1.4 on the Subject.

constantly involved with in the process of our lives (Cixous in: Sellers 1991:148; my emphasis).

So how to take Cixous' indications? Her own texts are strange, they tease the reader into their folds. They are not formulaic, nor do they offer precise dissections of problems with solutions proffered. With their musicality and mystery, they seduce the reader into listening. In offering no immediate solutions, they defer comprehension, thereby embodying the deconstructive concept of *différance*.

It occurs to me that the salient features of a *lecture féminine* could be reduced to two points: *how* and *what*. How does one read? If, up to now, one has read looking for understanding from a limited number of sources, *lecture féminine* opens up this practice to more sources. If works of music were previously read for aspects of structure, balance, and harmony, a *lecture féminine* might read them for myriad new aspects, such as how the notion of the composing subject manifests itself in a work. And how are they read? Teleologically, to end up at certain knowledge? How can any knowledge be new, if it was read to be found? Or to experience a work in a different way? "They do not fetishize... they observe, they approach" (LM:892).

And, what do we read? Only works in our canon? Susan Sellers, often quoted here, has this to say about *lecture féminine,* gleaned from her experiences in Cixous' seminars (Wilcox et al. 1990:192):

> Perhaps the best way to describe a 'feminine' reading is to say that it implies 'opening' the self to what it is the text is saying, even if this is puzzling or painful or problematic. It entails reading to see how a text is made, by exploring all the various resources for meaning a writer has at their disposal: the writer's intended meaning, as well as the 'other' meanings that contradict, complement, unsettle, or dislodge this meaning. It involves standing back from the text and looking at its overall construction; it entails reading at the level of the words themselves, at the level of the syntax, the syllables and letter-patterns, the rhythm and punctuation. It means asking who and what produced this text: and why? It means acknowledging that I as reader participate in the ongoing process of the text's creation; it means

recognizing that my reading is itself a product of certain questions, blind-spots, needs and desires, and that these motivations are constantly changing. The question of how we read includes the question of what we read.

Sellers, too, adds a notice on the consequences feminine reading has for writing:

> Blurring the rigid and, to me, absurd distinction between 'critical' and 'creative' writing, a 'feminine' writing entails relinquishing the pseudo-objectivity of conventional critical discourse and implicating ourselves as writers, accepting our role in the signifying process as well as the way language itself works on and shapes what we write (194).

Catherine Clément, in her joint work with Cixous, *The Newly Born Woman* (1986), described the necessity of struggling for a truly democratic transmission of knowledge with great subtlety:

> It is true that whole segments of knowledge are "trapped" in the dominant ideology, but still they are conveyed. There are, for example, Marxist historians; they teach history in a 'history' program. It is not because they are in a position of mastery within the teaching structure as it is now that the *content* of their knowledge goes hand in hand with ideology. The division is more complex: it is between the subject's position in relation to knowledge and *the specific effects of the knowledge itself.* The transmission is effective in any kind of structure; even if it is attenuated by the instructional system, it is not *wiped out* (142).

A theory of otherness that brings the body into play with the intellect, that questions the validity of the text, that poetically encourages a collective and respectful approach to reading with an abundance of interpretations: All of these notions and more are included in *lecture féminine.*

Cixous' approach might help us bridge the theoretical gap as we move from the autonomous work of music toward experiential media art. For, perception can happen with the mind, or perhaps with the body. More and more, neuroscience is encoding the bodily reactions and actions involved in reading. If *écriture féminine* writes the body, perhaps *lecture féminine* reads with the body, with the entire body.

I close with Cixous' words: "For us the point is not to take possession in order to internalize or manipulate, but rather to dash through and to 'fly' [*voler*: also, to steal]" (LM:887).

Figure 4 (above and below) - Cixous' Seminar
at the Collège international de philosophie, Paris, 2004

Corrections and questions regarding this text can be sent to: joyce@joyceshintani.com.

If you enjoyed this text, I would appreciate your honest evaluation in the form of a review on Amazon or Goodreads.com.

Thank you.
Joyce Shintani

4. Bibliography

n.d. = no date

Although it stops with the year 2000, the definitive annotated bibliography of Cixous' works and of works about her is compiled by Eddie Yeghiayan at the University of California Irvine http://sun3.lib.uci.edu/~scctr/Wellek/cixous/index.html, retrieved 11 Aug 2007.

There is an excellent bibliography for Julia Kristeva online at: http://ms.cc.sunysb.edu/~hvolat/kristeva/krist02.htm.

Barthes, R. (1967) "Death of the Author", R. Howard (trans.), Item 3 in *Aspen* no. 5+6, New York: Roaring Fork Press; accessible at http://www.ubu.com/aspen/aspen5and6/index.html retrieved 29 Aug 2007; also in *Image – Music – Text* (1977) S. Heath (trans), New York: Hill and Wang.

Berman, A. (1988) *From the New Criticism to Deconstruction. The Reception of Structuralism and Post-structuralism*, Urbana: University of Illinois Press.

Berman, M. (2000) *The Twilight of American Culture,* New York: Norton.

Bosma, H. (1997) *"Écriture féminine and Electrovocal Music"* abstract of unpublished manuscript for Feminist Theory and Music Conference FTM7 in Charlottsville VA in June 1997, available online http://www.hannahbosma.nl/paperFTM4.html retrieved 12 Sep 2007.

Briganti, C. and Davis, R. C. (1994) *The Johns Hopkins Guide to Literary Theory and Criticism*, Baltimore: Johns Hopkins University Press, pp. 162-164; cited in "Stanford Presidential Lectures and Symposia in the Humanities and Arts. Cixous, Hélène" http://prelectur.stanford.edu/lecturers/cixous/efcrit.html retrieved 3 Oct 2007.

Butler, J. (2004) *Undoing gender*, New York: Routledge.

_____ (1995) "Burning Acts, Injurious Speech" in Parker, A. and Kosofsky Sedgwick, E. (eds) *Performativity and Perfor-*

mance. *Essays from the English Institute*, New York: Routledge, pp. 197-237.
_____ (1993) *Bodies that Matter. On the Discursive Limits of "Sex"*, London: Routledge.
_____ (1990) *Gender Trouble*. *Feminism and the Subversion of Identity*, New York: Routledge.
Calle-Gruber, (2006) *Genèses, généalogies, genres. Autour de d'Hélène Cixous; [actes du colloque tenu à la Bibliothèque Nationale de France du 22 au 24 mai 2003]* [Genesis, Genealogies, Genres. Surrounding Hélène Cixous' Œuvre. Proceedings of the colloquium held at the French National Library from 22 to 24 May 2003], Paris: Galilée, Bibliothèque Nationale de France.
_____ (2002) *Du café à l'éternité: Hélène Cixous à l'œuvre*, Paris: Galilée.
_____ (ed) (2000) *Hélène Cixous, croisées d'une œuvre. Les secrets de l'archive*, Paris: Galilée Act of Colloquium 22-30 June 1998, Centre culturel international de Cerisy-la-Salle of same name. Many contributors, incl. Derrida, Schirag, Prenowitz Collection La Philosophie en Effet.
_____ and Germain, M. O. (eds) (2006) *Genèses Généalogies Genres. Autour de l'œuvre d'Hélène Cixous*, Paris : Galilée / Bibliothèque nationale de France.
Cixous, H. (2005) "Derrida", http://www.humanite.fr/node/320779, Journal l'Humanité 21.Jan.05.
_____ (2004) *The Writing Notebooks of Hélène Cixous*, Sellers, S. (ed), New York: continuum.
_____ (2002) *Manhattan. Lettres de la préhistoire* [Manhattan. Prehistoric Letters], Paris: Galilée.
_____ (2001) *Portrait de Jacques Derrida en Jeune Saint Juif,* Paris: Galilée, English Bie Brahic, B. (Trans.) (2004) *Portrait of Jacques Derrida As a Young Jewish Saint*, New York: Columbia University Press.
_____ (1998) *Stigmata: Escaping Texts*, New York: Routledge.
_____ (1998) "'Mamae, disse ele' or Joyce's second hand" ch. 7 in *Stigmata. Escaping texts*, London: Routledge.
_____ (1998) "'What is it o'clock?' *or The door (we never enter)"* ch. 5 in *Stigmata. Escaping texts,* London: Routledge.
_____ (1996) "Guardian of Language. An Interview with Hélène Cixous" by Kathleen O'Grady in *Women's educations des femmes* (12,4) Winter 1996-7, Canada, pp. 6-10. Available online http://bailiwick.lib.uiowa.edu/wstudies/cixous/ retrieved 11 Sep 2007.
_____ and Calle-Gruber, M. (1994) Photos de Racine Paris: des femmes ; English edition (1997e) *Rootprints. Memory and Life Writing,* Prenowitz, E. (Trans.), New York : Routledge.

_____ (1993a) *Beethoven à jamais, ou l'existence de dieu*, Paris: des femmes.
_____ (1993b) *Three Steps on the Ladder of Writing* Cornell, S. and Sellers, S. (trans.), New York: Columbia University Press; 3 lectures given in May 1990 at UCI.
_____ (1991) "Coming to Writing" in *"Coming to Writing" and Other Essays*, Jenson, D., Liddle, A. (eds) and Sellers, S. (trans.), Cambridge MA: Harvard University Press.
_____ (1980) Geschriebene Frauen – Frauen in der Schrift *Weiblichkeit in der Schrift*, Berlin: Merve pp. 22-57; "den Text würde ich auch gerne als Grundlage meines Vortrags nehmen"
_____ (1980) Wer singt? Wer veranlasst zu singen? in *Hélène Cixous. Weiblichkeit in der Schrift*, Berlin: Merve pp. 58-107.
_____ (1977) *Die unendliche Zirkulation des Begehrens. Weiblichkeit in der Schrift*, Berlin: Merve
_____ (1976) Schreiben, Feminität, Veränderung *Alternative 108/109. Zeitschrift für Literatur und Diskussion*, Berlin: Alternative Verlag pp. 134-154. German translation by Monika Bellan of an excerpt from "Sorties" in *La Jeune née* (1975). The title on the cover of this special issue of Alternative is "Das Lächeln der Medusa" [The laugh of the Medusa].
_____ (1976e) "The Laugh of the Medusa" [abbreviation LM in this text] (English translation) Cohen, K. and Cohen, P. (trans) in *Signs. Journal of Women in Culture and Society*, vol. 1, nr. 4, pp. 875-894, Chicago: University of Chicago Press.
_____ (1976s) "Le Sexe ou la tête?" in *Les Cahiers du GRIF*, October, Vol. 13, Paris, pp. 5-15. Text transcribed from a conversation between Hélène Cixous and the editors of *Les Cahiers du GRIF* (Groupes de Recherche et d'Information Féministe) which took place in Brussels during 1975.
_____ (1976l) *LA*, Paris : Gallimard.
_____ (1975) "Le Rire de la Méduse.' *L'Arc*, vol. 61, pp. 39-54 ; issue on "Simone de Beauvoir et la lutte des femmes" [Simone de Beauvoir and women's struggle].
_____ (1972) *Neutre*, Paris: Éditions Grasset.
_____ (1970) *Le Troisième corps*, Paris: Grasset. English (1999) *The Third Body*, Cohen, K. (trans), Evanston IL: Northwestern University Press.
_____ (1969) *Dedans*, Paris: Grasset.
_____ and Calle-Gruber, M. (1994) *Photos de Racine*, Paris: des femmes ; English edition (1997e) *Rootprints. Memory and Life Writing*, Prenowitz, E. (Trans.), New York : Routledge.
_____ and Clément, C., (1975) *La Jeune Née*, Paris: Union Générale d'Éditions, Band 984; English edition (1986) *The Newly Born Woman*, Wing, B. (trans), Minneapolis : University of Minnesota Press.

_____ Gagnon, M. and Leclerc, A. (1977) La venue à l'écriture *Venue à l'écriture, la,* Paris: Union générale d'éditions 3 essays. 1) HC, 2) Gagnon "Mon corps dans l'écriture", 3) Leclerc "La lettre d'amour", Série "féminin futur" dirigée par Catherine B. Clément et Hélène Cixous; collection 1018 dirigée par C. Bourgois
_____ and Sellers, S. (ed) (2004) *The writing notebooks of Hélène Cixous,* New York: Continuum.
Conley, V. A. (1984) *Hélène Cixous. Writing the Feminine,* London: University of Nebraska Press.
Cooper, S. (2000) "Bisexual Textual Economies. Reading Sexuality through Hélène Cixous's Writing" in Cooper, *Relating to Queer Theory. Rereading Sexual Self-Definition with Irigaray, Kristeva, Wittig and Cixous,* Bern: Peter Lang, pp. 187-207.
Cox, C. (2005) *"A la recherché d'une Musique Féminine"* in Dzuverovic, L., Neset, A. H., and Young R. (eds) *Her Noise,* catalog for the London exhibit, Newcastle: forma arts and media, pp. 9-13.
_____ (2003) "Wie wird Musik zu einem organlosen Körper? Gilles Deleuze und die experimentelle Elektronika" [How Do You Make Music a Body without Organs? Gilles Deleuze and Experimental Electronica] in Kleiner, S. and Szepanski, A. (eds) (2003) *Soundcultures. Über elektronische und digitale Musik* [Sound Cultures. On Electronic and Digital Music], Frankfurt: Suhrkamp, pp. 162-193.
Cox Lorraine, R. see under Lorraine.
Dame, J. (1994) "Unveiled Voices. Sexual Difference and the Castrato" in Brett et al. *Queering the Pitch,* pp. 139-154.
_____ (1994) *Het zingend lichaam. betekenissen van de stem in westerse vocale muziek [The Singing Body. Significance of the Voice in Western Vocal Music],* Kampen : Kok Agora.
Deleuze, G. and Guattari, F. (1980n) "Treatise on Nomadology. The War Machine" in *Mille Plateaux* (vol. 2 of *Capitalisme et Schizophrénie,* Paris: Minuit; English Edition (1987) *A Thousand Plateaus. Capitalism and Schizophrenia,* Massumi, B. (trans), London: Continuum, pp. 387-467.
Derrida, J. (1967) *De la grammatologie,* corrected English edition (1997e) translated by Spivak, G. C., Baltimore: Johns Hopkins University Press.
Fisher, C. (1988) *La cosmogonie d'Helene Cixous,* Amsterdam: Rodopi.
Gamble, S. (ed.) (2001) *The Routledge Companion to Feminism and Postfeminism,* New York: Routledge.
Goehr, L. (1998) *The Quest For Voice. On Music, Politics, and the Limits of Philosophy,* Oxford: Oxford University Press.

_____ (1992) *The Imaginary Museum of Musical Works. An Essay in the Philosophy of Music*, Oxford: Oxford University Press.
Graham, D., Wallis, B. (ed) (1993) "New Wave Rock and the Feminine" in *Rock My Religion. Writings and Art Projects 1965-1990*, Cambridge, MA: MIT Press, pp. 116-137.
Iitti, S. (2006) *The Feminine in German Song*, New York: Peter Lang.
Irigaray, L. (1991) Ethik der sexuellen Differenz, Frankfurt: Suhrkamp.
_____ (1985) "Any Theory of the 'Subject' Has Always Been Appropriated by the 'Masculine'" in Speculum. Of the Other Woman (G. C. Gill, trans) Ithaca (NY): Cornell University Press, pp. 133-146.
_____ (1979) "Eine bewegt sich nicht ohne die andere" in Freibeuter. Vierteljahreszeit-schrift für Kultur und Politik. Thema: Frauen in Gesellschaft. No. 2, Berlin: Freibeuter/Wagenbach, pp. 72-78.
_____ (1976) "Die Macht des Diskurses. Unterordnung des Weiblichen. Ein Gespräch" in Das Geschlecht, das nicht eins ist, Berlin: Merve pp. 70-88.
_____ (1976) Das Geschlecht, das nicht eins ist Waren, Körper, Sprache. Der ver-rückte Diskurs der Frauen, Berlin: Merve pp. 7-16.
_____ (1976) Ein anderer geschlechtlicher Körper, ein anderes Imaginäres Waren, Körper, Sprache. Der ver-rückte Diskurs der Frauen, Berlin: Merve pp. 17-24 Internationale Marxistische Diskussion 62.
_____ (1976) Macht des Diskurses/Unterordnung des Weiblichen Waren, Körper, Sprache. Der ver-rückte Diskurs der Frauen, Berlin: Merve pp. 25-41 Internationale Marxistische Diskussion 62.
_____ (1974) Speculum. De l'autre femme, Paris: Minuit; English edition Speculum Of the Other Woman (1985), Gill, G (trans) Ithaca (NY): Cornell University Press. Ives, K. (1996) *Cixous, Irigaray, Kristeva. The Jouissance of French Feminism*, Kidderminster: Crescent Moon Publishing.
Kristeva, J. (1987) "Talking about Polylogue" in Moi, T. (ed.) French Feminist Thought. A Reader, Oxford, New York: Blackwell.
_____ (1979) "Kein weibliches Schreiben? Fragen an Julia Kristeva" in Freibeuter. Vierteljahreszeitschrift für Kultur und Politik. Thema: Frauen in Gesellschaft. No. 2, Berlin: Freibeuter/Wagenbach, pp. 79-84.
_____ (1979) "Women's Time" in Warhol, R. R. and Herndl, D.P. (eds) Feminisms: An Anthology of Literary Theory and Criticism, New Brunswick: Rutgers U. Press, 1997, pp. 860-877.Lindhoff, L. (1995) *Einführung in die feministische Literaturtheorie*, Stuttgart: Metzler; 2nd edition (2003).

Lorraine, R. C. (2001) "Recovering Jouissance. Feminist Aesthetics and Music" in Pendle, K. (ed.) *Women and Music. A History of Feminist Aesthetics and Music* 2nd edition, Bloomington: Indiana University Press; first edition 1991.

MacArthur, S. (2002) *Feminist Aesthetics in Music*, Westport CT: Greenwood Press.

Madsen, P. (1994) "Toward A Feminine Form in Music. Pauline Oliveros' *Rose Moon*" in *Contemporary Music Forum. Proceedings of the Bowling Green State University New Music and Art Festivals 14 & 15. Paper Sessions*, volumes 5-6, pp. 5-14.

Marks, E. and De Courtivron, I. (eds.) (1980) *New French Feminisms. An Anthology*, New York: Schocken Books. Writings by de Beauvoir, Cixous, Leclerc, Groult, Herrmann, Duras, Parturier, Kristeva, Gauthier, Irigaray, Macciocchi, Wittig, and others.

Martin, S.-P. (1988) *Open Form and the Feminine Imagination. The Politics of Reading in Twentieth-Century Innovative Writing*, Washington D.C.: Maisonneuve Press.

Moi, T. (1999) *What is a Woman? And Other Essays*, Oxford: Oxford University Press.

_____ (ed.) (1987) *French Feminist Thought. A Reader*, Oxford: Basil Blackwell.

_____ (1985) *Sexual/Textual Politics. Feminist Literary Theory*, London: Routledge.

Negrón, M. (ed.) (1994) *Lectures de la Différence sexuelle. Textes réunis et présentés par Mara Negrón*, Paris: des femmes. Contains communications presented at colloquium at the Collège international de philosophie in Oct 1990.

Osinski, J. (1998) *Einführung in die feministische Literaturwissenschaft*, Berlin: Erich Schmidt Verlag.

Rambures, J.-L. de (1978) *Comment travaillent les écrivains*, Paris: Flammarion.

Reynolds, S. and Press, J. (1995) *The Sex Revolts: Gender, Rebellion, and Rock 'n' Roll*, Cambridge, MA: Harvard University Press.

Rieger, Eva (1992) "'I Recycle Sounds': Do Women Compose differently?" quoted in MacArthur, S. (2002) *Feminist Aesthetics in Music*, Westport CT: Greenwood Press, pp. 12-13.

Riley, T. (2004) *Fever: How Rock 'n' Roll Transformed Gender in America*, New York: St. Martin's Press.

Rossum-Guyon, F. and Díaz-Diocaretz, M. (eds) (1990) *Hélène Cixous. Chemins d'une écriture*, Saint-Denis: Presses Universitaires de Vincennes. Act of colloquium held in June 1987 in Utrecht.

Schmiedel, S. M. (2004) *Contesting the Oedipal Legacy. Deleuzean vs. Psychoanalytic Feminist Critical Theory*, Münster: Lit Verlag.
Sellers, S. (1996) *Hélène Cixous. Authorship, Autobiography and Love*, Cambridge UK: Polity Press
_____ (ed), (1994) *Hélène Cixous Reader*, London, New York: Routledge Foreword by Jacques Derrida, Preface by Hélène Cixous, Afterword by Mireille Calle-Gruber
_____ (1991) *Language and Sexual Difference. Feminist Writing in France*, New York: St. Martin's Press
_____ (ed), (1991) *Feminist Criticism: Theory and Practice*, New York: Harvester Wheatsheaf.
_____ (ed), (1988) *Writing Differences. Readings from the Seminar of Hélène Cixous*, New York: St. Martin's Press.
_____ (1988) "Conversations with Hélène Cixous and Members of the Centre d'Études Féminines" in *Writing Differences. Readings from the Seminar of Hélène Cixous*, New York: St. Martin's Press.
_____ and Blyth, I. (2004) *Hélène Cixous. Live Theory*, New York: Continuum.
_____ (ed) and Cixous, H. (2004) *The writing notebooks of Hélène Cixous*, New York: Continuum.
Shiach, M. (1991) *Hélène Cixous. A Politics of Writing*, London, New York: Routledge
Shintani, J. (2015) "Bridging the Gap: Gerhard Stäbler" in P. Attinello (ed.) *live · the opposite · daring. Gerhard Stäbler. Music, Graphic, Concept, Event*. Büdingen: Pfau, pp. 108-123.
_____ (2010) "New Musicology and the Composing Subject. Theory-*Métissage* with a Look at Gerhard Stäbler" in M. Grabócz and M. Solomos (eds.) *Revue Filigrane. Musique, Esthétique, Sciences, Sociéte, N° 11. New Musicology. Perspectives critiques*, Sampzon: Delatour, pp. 89-105.
Showalter, E. (ed.) (1985) *The New Feminist Criticism. Essays on Women, Literature, and Theory*. New York: Pantheon.
Simon, J. (2004) *Rewriting the Body. Desire, Gender and Power in Selected Novels by Angela Carter*. Frankfurt: Peter Lang.
Wardle, C. H. (2007) *Beyond 'écriture féminine'. Repetition and Transformation in the Prose Writing of Jeanne Hyvrard*, London: Manley Publishing.
Wilcox, H., McWatters, K., Thompson, A., and Williams, R. (eds) (1990) *The Body and the Text. Hélène Cixous, Reading and Teaching*, Hertfordshire: Harvester Wheatsheaf.
Wittgenstein, L. (1921) *Tractatus logico-philosophicus*. Frankfurt: 4th Suhrkamp edition (1988).

Worth, S. (2001) "Feminist Aesthetics" in Gaut, B. and McIver Lopes, D. (eds.) (2001) *The Routledge Companion to Aesthetics,* London: Routledge.